SANDRA

SIMONDS

TRIPTYCHS

Wave Books   *Seattle*   *New York*

Published by Wave Books

www.wavepoetry.com

Copyright © 2022 by Sandra Simonds

All rights reserved

Wave Books titles are distributed to the trade by
Consortium Book Sales and Distribution

Phone: 800-283-3572 / SAN 631-760X

Library of Congress Cataloging-in-Publication Data

Names: Simonds, Sandra, author.

Title: Triptychs / Sandra Simonds.

Description: First Edition. | Seattle : Wave Books, [2022]

Identifiers: LCCN 2022020013

ISBN 9781950268696 (hardcover)

ISBN 9781950268689 (paperback)

Subjects: LCGFT: Poetry.

Classification: LCC PS3619.I5627 T75 2022 | DDC 811/.6—dc23

LC record available at https://lccn.loc.gov/2022020013

Designed by Crisis

Printed in the United States of America

9 8 7 6 5 4 3 2 1

First Edition

Wave Books 104

For Ezekiel   *and*   *Charlotte*

How are you going to trap reality?
How are you going to trap appearance
without making an illustration of it?

—Francis Bacon

TRIPTYCHS

I Gave Birth   In Another   Era

Woke to the "mean
  error" of birds
squawking inside
the scorched-gray-
 black polyphony of what
 happens when we lose
the terminology
 to determine how bad
things really are. Was
  there no way to
puncture the ago-
  nizing film
 keeping us all corralled
here? I looked through
  the window—be-
wildering axiom,
condition, assumption—
  I looked at the dwarf
orange tree, fruiting
  sour fruit incessantly.

Suppose it is possible
to be in three
  states of error
at once and in each place
  to think three things
 and in each thing
to feel a different version
of the salted wind as you
  are walking along
the high sea cliff.

Take, for example,
  apricots that have
  been gen-
  etically bred
to amplify the length of
time their fragrance stays
  in the crisp air
of the cadaverous super-
market, just long
  enough to
  place them
in your cart
and think to yourself,
the world is good.

You may be very lonely
at this point. The grocery
  clerk scans
the apricots and asks you
a few questions to which
the answers are
always "no."

"When will it all
be over?" asks
the griever, who's
a very small child
in the room
we have painted
Amalfi blue
but have not
yet filled with
sea-themed
decor. How much
of a garden's
design is made
more pleasing
through negative
space? Across
from the entry
for "grief"
is "grenade,"
which derives
from the Old
French word
for pomegranate.
Why do I
write poetry?
Because I don't
know what it
means to live
anymore—other
than the shapes
left behind.
Why do I write
poetry? Be-
cause I want
to drown.

Bildungsroman

Grabbed a hole.
Grabbed Mother.
Was abandoned.
Saw green light.
Was grief.
Was stellar in algebra.
Studied.
Learned collapse.
Practiced collapse.
Memorized collapse.
Saw red light.
Got awarded for collapse.
Was lonely.
Learned fields.
Practiced fields.
Memorized fields.
Smoked in fields,
emaciated.
Stole stickers.
Stole pencils.
Saw aqua light.
Stole eyeliner
Stole eyeshadow.
Left everything.

Ran away.
Came back.
Absconded.
Flirted. Skinned
my knees.
Was brutal.
Was beyond.
Was lured.
Was yelled at.
Took flights across
continents alone.
Memorized books.
Became a highly
skilled reader.
Earned awards.
Went back to the dry
fields and smoked.
Zoned out plenty.
Gravitated
toward criminals.
Saw orange light.
Criminals turned my
body into a crime scene.
Saw white light.
Commuted more.
Grabbed another hole.
That wasn't it.
Remembered what?
What was possible.
That wasn't it.
Became sick again.
That wasn't it.
Left one bad state
for another.

Practiced libraries.
Memorized libraries.
Mastered libraries.
Grabbed at a mother.
Grabbed at nothing.
Grabbed a black hole.
Gave birth.
Held on.
Breast-fed.
Commuted.
Traveled widely
with libraries memorized.
Amassed nothing.
An infant tugged at my
nipple.
Became sick.
Made smoothies.
Created dioramas.
Bought a house.
Was choked.
Gave birth again.
Almost bled to death.
Stayed in the hospital.
Recovered.
Took pharmaceuticals.
Went back to work.
Made more dioramas.
Saw purple light.
Went back to bed.
Made mac and cheese.
Commuted. Amassed
nothing. Became sick
again. Took more
pharmaceuticals.
Bought tent.
Bought sleeping bag.
Went camping.
Looked at the stars.
Made love.
Grabbed another hole.
That wasn't it.
Remembered what?
What was possible.
That wasn't it.

Reading The Bell Jar

When Esther Greenwood
is almost raped, why
can't she connect
what happened
to her downward
spiral: from throwing

designer clothes
off the hotel
balcony to her
unwashed hair, electro-
shock therapy

and worse? "Slut,"
the guy kept saying.
"Slut slut slut,
where's my
diamond, Slut?"

*

In 6th grade science class
there was a boy who
lit the hair
of girls on fire.
The science teacher

laughed *ha ha ha*
(she didn't believe us

when we told her)
ha ha ha until the smell

of Heidi's burned
braid mixed with
the chalk

powder that fell off
the enormous grave-
green board.

In Everglades

It rained all day.
Then, I read your poetry.

I lied twice.
First, when I told
you I wasn't afraid of rain
and then when I put
it in this poem. So, I
unfolded the piece
of paper where
the poem was and wrote
a true story: eight or ten
vultures on top
of a Corolla pecking
at a black tarp
the national park
provides their visitors.

I texted Alex, *vultures
are the bird form of roaches.*
Then, one of them
looked at me.

"There were vultures
everywhere, in
the swimming pool
vomiting, shitting,
blood blood blood.
It was gross," said Mrs.
Delamo who bought
a $700K vacation
home in West Palm
where the birds invaded.
It wouldn't stop looking.
All the other birds
were pecking away
at the tarp to get to
the windshield wipers,
which, apparently, give
off the scent of a carcass
when the plastic melts
in the sun. "Save me save
me save me," I said
to the vulture, but it
wouldn't look away.

National Park

My name is Esther
Greenwood. Sometimes,
I get a bad idea

and follow
through on it. That's
the difference between me

and other people. Other
people get distracted by
roasting a chicken or
watching TV,
but I am carnal.

I know the difference
between killing
yourself and stepping
down the spiral
staircase into the cellar
of the self, that really
meaty, stringy place
wrapped in shadows,
booming with an arterial
pulse so that if you
were to kill it, it
would mean something.

Now, look at me.
Look at the mirror
I'm holding up.
You can smash it.
There's another face
behind it, and another
one behind that. Just like

stars, they are endless
and stretch obliviously
in their cold calculations.

It is Christmas Eve,
so go ahead, smash it.
I'm sure someone
out there
is in love with me.

Gong!

The man from Paros
who lives beyond
the temple of Artemis
takes a high fever.
When they inject
me with a cerulean
anesthetic, I become
the mint I planted
between the jasmine
and swimming
pool. On the sixth
day, the man from
Paros is delirious.
When I wake, the nurse
gives me a painkiller.
Winter was like spring
and spring like winter.
On the eighth day,
the man from Paros
dreams in turquoise,
of the nodes on the body
where sea and sky
entwine, dreams of
his mother who bakes
octopus. I stand up.
I faint. On the tenth
day, the man from Paros
believes he will die
and is now very
angry at himself
for keeping secret
his love for a man
in the next village,
but the man from Paros
cannot move and must
send a messenger.
I get up, ask my husband
for the mascara in my
purse. On the sixteenth
day, the man from
Paros receives no
word from his

Gong!

"I cry," Jane Eyre says,
"because I am miserable,"
but what could she know
of town hall meetings
on climate crisis, work-
flow, the technological
sophistication of our new
lingo—content strategists,
reaching out (did
Ms. Eyre reach out
to Rochester or to her
little friend who died of
consumption? Jane
held the girl all night
and in the morning
she was dead)—calls
to action, optimizing,
becoming "impactful"?
Jane's world revolved
around so little and yet,
it was a life. Newest
version of the world:
hurricanes that obliterate;
investors who come in,
buy the islands cheap.
I Dub Thee la ti
Landlord of the Under-
world and you can
pick up your laurels
at the Teller of Bones.
Baudelaire's family was so
annoyed he was a poet
they sent him on a long
sea voyage from Calais
to Calcutta. He hated
everyone on the boat
except Jane Eyre.
He liked her because
she was ugly and read
books. "A poem," he
said to her as they
crossed the Horn

Gong!

We often say the sun
is *over there*; he walked
over the hill with a hand-
ful of figs. To wander
helplessly into the artist's
fist. No wonder he
couldn't find the king in
this painting of the former
world. You will feel
the ecclesiastical
floodplain, clay,
heartbreak. Some people
with a psychological
disorder eat soil.
And some, in grief,
pull hair from their head
and eat it. In another
life, I pulled hair
from my head.
Grief begins so full
of water and ends
saying farewell to
the sour, wild pears
of another island, for-
saken, the core shaken.
Don't forget rivulets
of fluid down your leg
after sex, the sensuous
smell of musical
geraniums after a long
rain, two owls
crisscrossing the green-
gray sky. He roamed
and roamed. What is
growing from my little
palm tree? Long,
outrageous fronds!
Get back where you be-
long! Now his back is to
the artist, his long
scarlet cloak mocking
the attenuation. The man

source of Eros.
When I return
home, I urinate
blood. On
the twentieth day,
he has a visionary dream:
it is not the world
of Greece in 500 BCE
but rather our world,
dolphins with plastic
in their intestines, an ice
shelf slamming into
the sea, Black boys shot
in the street, and he tries
to explain this to his
mother, but she
is confused for what does
"plastic" or "gun"
mean in ancient Greek?
Why are the rivers beige?
Why is the sea tobacco-
brown? Why are weeds
growing through my palms?
I take the pain
medicine, start an email
to my estranged mother.
Delete it.
On the twenty-
fourth day, the man
from Paros hears back
from his love who
has given the messenger
one fig. Hippocrates
says nothing more
about the man
except that he lived.

of Africa, "can trip
the real." "I refuse
anything and every-
thing that is prejudicial
to my personal liberty,"
Jane said. "I will have
the world," Charles said.
"Or nothing," Jane
finished. When they
stopped in Mauritius,
Jane and Charles found
some literary people,
smoked hashish, made
love again and again
and refused
to go on, so they
bribed the sea
captain and some-
how returned to France.
A love like this can't
fit into cramped
medieval streets.
Things grow tedious
inside sunsets.
Why, he wondered,
after such a splendid
adventure, had
Jane fled? Simple:
the pleasure of
annihilation can only
sustain the duration
of three suns, three
isometric chords,
then gone. "I cry,"
Charles Baudelaire says,
"because I am miserable."

with perfect Latin,
walking away with a lan-
tern, snake, angel, lark.
Remember, my dear,
when things weren't so far
away that the imagination
got a crack at it?
Something like children
whacking a piñata
with a baseball bat,
candy pouring from
the unicorn's torn
rib cage. Could this
be the golden tree?
Now forget the man in
the painting. Neuron
mapping looks a lot
like freeze, thaw, alluvial
fans—but knowledge,
you know, isn't only info.
In Thásos, the wife of
Epicrates caught a wicked
fever from her grief, wept
and laughed, wrapped
herself up, sometimes
talked of blackberries,
alone, pulling out
her hair. Ninth day:
random babbling.
Fourteenth day: breaths
short like the sound of
insects. Seventeenth day:
inscrutable to everything.
Twentieth day: loss
of voice. Twenty-
first day: died.

Now That You're Dead,

.....Days of idols................
......of verdant shoots.........
......of syllables...................

.....Days of toxic waves.....
.....of the vocative..............
..........leashed....................

..........Days of incision.......
.......of endless growth.......
.....of misinformation.........

......Days of collaborators..
...............of silk..................
...............of the volcanic....

........Days repeating..........
......molten, squinting.........
......Days of copyright........

.........Days scathing...........
................denounced........
..Days characterized by....

I'm Observing

The chaotic chop
of storm light
tangled in salt water.

The "real being"—
feeling, talking, living.

A parrot flies
through the front door

of your wooden house
on stilts which sits
at the Gulf's
decrescent edge.

An elegy catches
in the parrot's
emerald feathers, so you
look
to the sea's shadows

scattering the snowy
dunes, turtles, and fronds.

Great Bodies of Water

Bodies of microplastics
in the indistinct chop

making their way farther
from flags, personalities,

and totems. Your eyes repeat
the landscape in equal

calculations of air
quality and awe.

Weather patterns sicken.
The soil sickens.

The water is thick
with blighted clocks, with

the accumulation of pock-
marked goods, the salt

gnawing down the useless
toy's plush bereavement.

With Joy

Night will fall
over my plate
of extraordinary
macarons, the peach
color will bleed into
the moon and maybe
a roach will scurry
from under the kitchen
sink and run over
the smooth egg
white top of those
confections, its
antennae dipping
into the rose
buttercream.
Jackpot! But
who's counting?
It scuttles to
the black square
of poison. When
I asked my husband
if he thought
the macarons were
good, he said, "no,
they're not good,
they're an experience."
I walked to the swim-
ming pool, dipped
my hands into
the night water,
and could feel some-
thing amniotic. It
was getting cold.
I could feel a chill
coming from the
underworld. Still,
I wanted to get in.
It was so dark
and calm. My
phone chimed
and my friend
texted, *the gangrene
of imperial decline
is setting in*.

With No

You do not
have to be gorgeous
to make pastel
meringues. You
only need a genuine
desire to take
your mind off
the world and supreme
focus on the super-
fine sugar as, teaspoon
by teaspoon,
you pour it into
the white froth
that turns
marshmallowy,
the way shelf-
clouds say
"it is time,"
and soon you
are driving
right past
the barrier
of tiny particles,
gas, water
droplets—
oh, all of it spins
and spins,
doesn't it?

Joy

Day will break
to the grating sounds
of a leaf blower
and a yapping dog.
I could plunge
into the bathtub
of Epsom salts
and lavender drops,
walk naked
to the fridge, open it
(waft of chemicals
and hormones
from the cold air),
lift the aluminum
foil off the green
bowl, and four
egg yolks stare
back at me like
a goblin. What
are you looking
at? Am I me?
I could turn
you into custard
if I wanted to,
could throw
you in the trash.
I have complete
control over
your destiny.

Now

As in emergence, the trip-
tych played all day,
diseased, phantas-
magorically, in
the car, in the blank
categorical, which was
work, work, work, through
the deep channels
of the grocery store that
involved gallons and
gallons of orange juice, it
played and played, an in-
strument with neither
beginning nor end, letters
unraveling in the black
strumming beyond
ordinary air so she held
onto the gossamer,
the viscous transitory
that bent history
like a frond that she
knew was a warped
trap, but why should
she care getting an
email from the novelist
between aisles, "you are
the spitting image of my
dead sister," the woman in
the red apron told her
and handed her the book
her dead sister wrote.
At home, she read
the book, its New
Age discom-
bobulations, meticulously
following the author's
search for Dion
Fortune, her pains-
taking documentation,
(trips to the UK,
interviews with people
who knew Dion, letters
etc.) but the lamentation
or doppelgänger or
ghost bore no fruit.

Wait

"The Museum of an Ex-
tinct Race. Did
you know about this?"
"No, I didn't know."
"Me neither." Exorbitant
simulacra—not a lie.
"It's shocking. Hitler
wanted to turn
the entire city of Prague
into this museum.
They were cataloguing
the books and all
of that." "I kind of
want to change
the channel." "No,
don't change it yet."
"I thought the Nazis
burned books."
"They did that
too. They catalogued
them and burned them.
They did both." I fell
asleep, fell into
(stage of) (entry)
dreamlife-half-con-
cealed—it (what was
it?) looks at the past
and present (sees
the same monuments).
What doesn't it see?
Tablecloths, wineglasses,
a sport's medal.
Progress (vanishes
with it). Shadow
(performs infinitely).
The sun is left-justified
and I am maddening,
haunted like cheeks.

For Last Year

In 1839, a rage for
tortoises overcame Paris.
Shortly after, an absolute
wonder became part of
history—the Crystal
Palace. "Dream" is used
411 times in *The Arcades
Project*; "history" 348.
Divide dream by
history, you get con-
volutions, residues
of utopia, the imaginary
number *e*, radicals,
negative fractions. News
of the palace brought
sheer delight to people.
Sheet glass, triangular
prisms, paths of light
through endless panes.
The sun is said to murder
dreams. I woke
with *The Quest for Dion
Fortune* in my lap.
On the facing page,
she had just seen
the vulturine devouring
of her city. Nothing left
but wreckage, meditations
and her black hair
in the bombed-
out atmosphere.
I was searching
for something, too.
Was I really her sister?
The lifeless? I wanted
to love you so much.

And the Days

Off the gridded
landscape, unraveling
        palindromes—
thinking
    of your dirty apart-
ment, box
of Special K [ripped
open on the ironing
        board—[they
flee at
 once in [the homophonic
substitutions and   [I
cultivate red chili
peppers,   where I laid
the harvest   on
    the lines between
plaintext and
ciphers
and they glowed
forensically.   You
could see the   [graves
stretch from   ozone layer
to tears in   [correct
numerical
sequence.   Drone
footage, [denatured,
the   great eyeball
of   machine [learning
to think as an
unblinking [predator,
as off-
on patterns   in
the contaminated [chaos
atmosphere—O   O   O
lovely, lovely bridge!

Shall Be Filled

[Speechless
couplets,   [what
  [did
   you
  make of
   the
     morning
inside the work-
flow]
        [flow
of the unreal]
      followed]
     [after you
have slept
all the   way
[through
  [the typography of
  [a trance
  of stars primeval in-
  side the teleported flesh
of each word]
      hazy material
you] transpose
or   transcribe?

I go] to the coffee
shop with
my cyclonic hair]
  alephs tied
in a knot] of figure 8s
lovely with a scrunchie
and I am happy
and order]
  an espresso
  and when the vulture
  lands on
  the grate
  across from
  my round table,
it becomes
  prophecy, an
  eclipse, in excess
  of spirit.

With Music

Like imprisoning]
a pressing need],
  you long to die]
    deeper
  than the sea peripheries
  with syllogistic surf
unorganized], passed
  over, rhapsodic in ion,
rhizome. One or
two] particles
  crystalize
in the radon shrubs. She
sauntered toward]
  the mountain; she
believed   it would
form]   a   dream,
a dream]   form
  engulfed by crypts].

"You feast on
the dead," I say.

It pulls a stringy
  tendon from
  the carcass
with its curved beak.

"No," he says,
"that's what poets do."

Let's Make

Pyres of brush
as anagram
of spontaneous com-
bustion, cloud
filling with wind
vectors, blasts
of char in my a-
orta, aerial fuels
how feelings
are an anchor
point on the
aspect, a single
tree, dead.
You were
the wild mech-
anism of the
vortex column
ascending through
a crown of
pines and blinding
the absolute
forbs, O mol-
ecules of blue
echo-locution
ground down
to stumps, for-
give me, I built
our love on
the fire line
between stra-
ta, the grasses
smoldering, ta
ta, my radiant
burn, you're the a-
pex, a charisma, se-
ed, Seer, Edenic
source text, ex-
it, woo
wound round
woe the two-
way radio waves
a fre-

The Water

A phantom
tracking the trip-
tych as pivot as
hydra flows
into hydro, it is my
personal theory of dis-
persion, sensory
overload used for
CIA experiments,
said one tremendous
wave to the next tre-
mendous wave that
came from thousands
of miles away, and
the first raised its voice,
as the second lowered
its voice and so on
and so forth and the
waves had a long
conversation with each
other, talked of what they
had lost, "have you left
anything in the world you
didn't wash away
by flood?" asked
the first wave.
"I have been burned
by the vapor
of many stars," replied
the second. "It is
a sort of sensory
deficiency they
suffer from," said
the first wave,
and the two waves
softly decayed
on the stretched
beach and they
could tell from the smell
of the sand
in the desert
that it was spring,

Turn Black

He told the story of
a hang glider who lost
his arm in 1998
not flying but
rather hopping
freights full
of cattle, trains trem-
bling with agitated
meat that would
not accept the adverse
conditions of their
demise, would not
accept their direction
of travel, and when
the man returned home
several months later
to his northern town
of aurora borealis,
huckleberries,
and hang gliders,
all his hang glider
friends had died due
to the defective
wings the company
had manufactured,
so we can see
this irony as mythos
on the fringe
of wind, that they
died in the latent
tower's downdraft,
in the deep cyclonic
ice, in the super
cooled remnants where
there remains a dense,
vigorous orb, an
iridescence, a cadence
that wraps the flagrant
urge eclipsed
by bites, a spectrum
of trauma-in-
duced reckoning.

quency never
quenched.
It is not me
searing on
the scaffold,
It is not me in-
side the excruciating
landscape's crux
and hex, I cannot
hold you dear
anymore, dear
tangential rope,
but what bright
christenings you
bring into swirling
conflagrations
red flags flapping
in the red fire
where the terrible
climactic descent
is dissected by
an atmospheric
death, an apotheosis
of form retracing
one more minute,
one more minute
the guru says,
torching as vo-
luptuous under-
burn, tender
water erasing
the rocks, tender,
tenderer water
erasing the granite.

the way sound
fluctuates almost
indefinitely,
and they felt
the two sides of
water wrap
around the birds
they could hear
and the oranges
ripening on the trees
more inland
and the gentle
frenzy of bees
and the little
girl walking
toward a mirage,
passing the mirage
into real water
and they could
reach very far
into her little
iris and could
see the entire
ocean in the back-
ground which was
the birthplace
of waves, the little
girl, and the story,
a generative
repetition
as the little girl
picked the fruit
and ate it quietly
by herself.

Where was
the man's arm?
He knocked on a hex-
agonal pat-
tern, I mean
he knocked on the door
of what falters,
I mean he knocked
on the door of the poly-
phonic, on what
cannot resonate or est-
ablish itself
in one eloquence,
their mouths, ears,
eyes full of graupel
and graupel on
their tongues as a
charm, as language
spiraling through
waves, fire, centuries
toward earth, turning
round and around
as mechanism, as
phenomenon, *how*
lucky I am, thinks
the man, *I would like*
an omelet and coffee,
thinks the man who
is now content to fade
instead of the others'
manifold omen, a lull
so turbulent—
I fold in.
I fold in.

The Poet / Enters through / The Subjunctive Mood

"If I were to keep acting."
"What do you mean?"
"I would just, you know,
pretend metaphors
weren't burned tips."
We sat in the orbis,
sat on the com-
bustable yet debonair
green. I, who dedicated
my life to art beyond
the penultimate.
Needed so much.
Sat with you.
Fuck the moon
with its love triangles.
Sat with you. Oblong,
mandatory. The forest
paths barked in the blank
atmosphere. Did these
spheres hate me so much
they were willing to cut
me in half? How did it
come to this? Was
shivering, melodious,
neurologically divergent
from the source material.
Wrote in my journal:

Orbis finiens: the horizon.
Orbis signifer: the zodiac.
Orbis, pars (*terrae*): a zone.

All your skinny notes
crammed in the margins
of the book you studied
endlessly. What is known
comes too late
and not for lack
of intelligence, this barely
perceptible touch.
The note on Sirius.
They are hard to make
out, my love, and I think
we are both always
on the brink of losing
something imported
from another textual
graveyard? Plague?
you asked. *Lucifer?*
A cold winter?
you wondered.
The Consolation of
Philosophy? One can
grow crazy with notes,
quaver, semi-
breve, trilling but not in-
different. You drove
to school to teach
and every day was
a good one (even
when a student
showed up at cross-
country practice
hungry), or so you
said. Every day for me
was text with no
annotation. But
I was noting things too:
The girl who made a video
called, "How I mani-
fested being on *The Today*
Show." I was arranging
what I took in, my vision
a lemon tree growing—

Turn your pockets
inside out
as you pass
that haunted house, so
phantoms won't follow
you down the road
to where my son
practices "Dona
nobis pacem" with
his violin teacher
and the neighbor's
kids are playing tag
with my daughter.
Climb into
your new voice.
My new voice says,
"look around
and wait for something
axial and pulmonary
to fill the garden." Watch
the kids' grandmother
cover a baby
moccasin with a terra-
cotta pot. "Will you kill
it for me?" she asks.
"I will not."

the thorns un-
believable—I can see
them from the dining
room table—terrific,
contrapuntal, shrill.

Sketches

Erasing the granite
with each step, the pack
mules hauled saws,
rope, food, gin,
and medicine over
boulders, toward
the grove of incense
cedars for the factory
had sent the men
and each man needed
a salary, $3 for food
and drink, and when
they finally reached
6,000 feet they found
a river and one of the men
poured river water over
his head and his sweat
mixed with the river
water. The man felt
uneasy, for he had seen
Sirius rise in the liquid
sky and he knew that star
meant fever, madness,
and trouble for the entire
party. The mules'
heads shot back
and forth spooked by,
what he reckoned,
was a bear in the cold
brush. I woke in
the middle of the night,
read about a mass
shooting, looked for
the shooter's mani-
festo, couldn't find
it online, took a pill
and returned to bed.
The man had good
instincts and knew
that to chop down
the cedars would
bring him nothing

For My Sweetheart

More by herself
than she ever imagined,
one platelet behind
the next, mov-
ing like sacral crystals
down the dense
arc of flickering
syncope, moving
through the mazed
vessels of a torn text.
A vertigo over-
came her, became
her own pulped
murmur of electrical
touch. She in-
verted. That's
what happens when
the crux comes
forward, announces
itself and lays
claim to the real.
Touch me at each
rhapsodic point,
and I will tell
the story of how
I broke. Was a vase
glued back to-
gether. Feel each
crack with your
forefinger, feel
the ventricles
branch, pathways
to the owl, long, black
talons, eyes deep
chambers, how I chopped
down its tree to save my
own house. Crane. Men.
Driveway. Payment.
Runic lumber
hauled away.
It has been six days
since the Dog Star

The Drunk

I fold the pamphlet
and put it in my
pocket. It seems
I am not an alcoholic,
after all. I'm simply
wanting access
to the dappled
interior, wanting
to channel the sparks
of Orion, the iris; Or-
pheus had a mysterious
cult: *Attend muses,*
to my sacred song!
My children are out
getting frozen yogurt
so that I can write
this poem. Blown-
up Swimming Pool
Unicorn, you
are scary! Your
eyes are unreal!
You dazzle me!
You are a rock star!
But your coruscant
colors don't belong
here. Beyond
you, there's a vineyard,
time's throat, a grape
stomped on by peasants,
the medieval wall
some poor man
decided he would
scale. He was going
to kill the landlord
and run. He resolved
to do it and you know
what? He was going
to get away with it
because he had
accomplices, not
friends exactly, but
people whom he could

but heartache.
He had never
used a pencil
for he could neither read
nor write, but he knew
about Sirius and his life
took a sharp right
turn one month after
the party felled twenty
cedars in the Dog Days
of summer, 1851.
The word "codex," comes from
the Latin word for tree trunk
I typed as a student in the
dendritic lecture
hall. Cumberland,
England (1563), a
shepherd takes shelter
under an ash tree.
When lighting strikes,
the tree is upturned
and he notices a black
substance clinging to its
roots. What good
are instincts if you
don't follow them?
He draws his name
on the white stones of his
house with the black
substance and eventually
it is encased in wood,
pencils dispersed to school
children across the world.
There is a small point
of graphite stuck under
my skin just above
the knee. In 6th grade
I accidentally stabbed
myself. How does
a child accidentally
stab herself? It didn't
bleed but the mark
has remained (axons
terminate) here
for forty years.

has risen through
the tight throat
of sky. You say
you will not listen
to astrology but
in this garden
of our meteors'
octaves between
eggplant and sage,
what if it's me who
has changed? What if
the notion I must be be-
loved topples
and what if the incense
accidentally burns
down the house into
a small collection
of items thrown
into a backpack?
Paisley scarf, two
pencils, a bra, some
figs and off to Canada
or to the Peru
I found on a postcard
of Machu Picchu,
and in fine cursive:
Mother, you must be
surprised that
I sent home
so much laundry.
Tell Tommy
we miss him and
we will be back
in about two
weeks' time.
They would,
I think, get on
without me.
I sit in the yard
wasted, clutching
a pencil. I sketch
a robin. A jay.
But I never see
the owl again.
She will never return.

count on and a vision,
powered with
the very wine he was
meant, for his entire life
from birth to death,
death to birth, to produce.
But he said *no*.
No to the vision,
but also to the confines.
César Vallejo hated
the drunkenness
of his countrymen.
Who could blame him?
He wanted them to revolt;
didn't want to see them
placated by the vine
in the evening hours
when they believed
nothing could
ever change.
How am I going
to placate you,
Lover, grape, erotic
half, how am going
to distill this poem
for you? How am I,
Princess of the Nude,
of the Night Sky,
of Felled Trees
supposed to exist
as draft, as
chamomile, balm
in this sweet night
of cicadas and frogs?
The last tomato
of August ripens
on the vine
and I will pluck it
from its swollen
branch and will make
love all night.
I will suck it all,
seed, pulp, and juice
to ignite, accelerate
my glorious flesh.

I Sang

A body in service.
A body in service
to hell. A body in
service to work.
A body to work
in service. A body
in service to serve.
A body to serve
the furnaces
of hell. A body
in service of hell
to the furnaces.
A body that must ring
to the frequency
of the superpower.
Drone-slender body
enough to reproduce
itself in the eyes
of the body-possible,
perverse and framed
by corruption
and spun out from this
scenario of overflows.
Or a body slender
enough to squeeze
through these iron bars.
What pound the flesh?
I've forged.
Instantaneous sand.
Instantaneous dirt.

A Song

What is it with these
books? They don't say
anything about
the politics I'm feeling.
I've been looking
for hours. They don't
say anything about
my body, that it is heavy,
40 years old. That my
period is coming or
maybe not. They don't say
anything about the blood
that fell out of me
onto the hospital floor
after giving birth
to my second child.
They don't say anything
about the drives
back and forth
from one state
to the other
just to make money,
to keep going. They don't
say anything about
the time that was robbed
or the drugs taken
just to avoid
looking directly
into the sun. What is it
with these books?
I have been reading
them all day.
My mouth is dry.
My throat hurts.
Maybe I have swallowed
too many lies.
At the ossified
university all the
ossified professors
go on defending
the pillars of their
ossified institutions

With the Dead

Dear SANDRA
SIMONDS,

Barclays values

your opinion

in helping

us continue

to improve

the products

and services

we offer. We

welcome your

feedback. We

are here to

serve you. We

hope you will

join us.

while their students
are left to stare down
the future like animals in
razed woods. What is it
with these books?
My mouth hurts.
My throat hurts.
I am such a bloody being,
so full of blood inside
of me, outside
of me, in-between
me and other people.
Bloody and culpable
and capable of murder
or suicide. What is it
with these books?
They say nothing
about my body or mind.

March Pandémie
(including nested play,
a reminiscence, and
light entertainment)

. . . but what if I'm just a
loser

who has read too much?
(Duck

out of the violence,
don a mask

given to you by your ex's
new wife
with absolute contempt.)

Don't read
the Internet today
with its echo-locutions.
Really demeaning

text from a friend
I'm so glad you're

in therapy; looking
at the air plants in glass

bulbs, how they
harmonize with heaven's

hum, its
humid, bom-
bastic quietude.

Stevedores, Sallie Mae,
the long decline

of the preposterous

new century unraveling
(same as the last song),

except reversible. Turned
toward the fre-
quency of Roman
numerals

and junk bonds. Riot
town. Stashing
some dough under a dirty

pillow. Coins carry a lust
that's hermeneutical

and their stern
faces sting.

Bleating acceptance,
the clock does what it can
to dress you for strong-

willed accomplishment.
And isn't that
what they wanted?

"Tell us about your
work." Bitch, not again.

A cheap body is still
a body. A cheap
treasure—well, that's
another story.

If the clock doesn't go off
and you stay in bed

either masturbating

or looking at the ferns
or wrapped
in another body

with less of an emergency

system, the circuitry
jumping up to make
the coffee black and
drinking it from

the perforated cup, there
may be a tremble or
reckoning. On the lyric's
limit? Rolls

off my hungry lips. When
in doubt,
call Mother who will
chew you out

or your sister wedged into
that bourgeois
nightmare. Give me your
hands and go.

Hey there, Greenery,
old friend.
Systematically dire
display

of affection—could
be a contagion. Little
apprentice. Oh
performative
grief! (which we must be
either the subject of
or subjected to).

This is my memoir.
These statements—
all true, *promise*.

Bleed me into spring
like a period juggling
the body: I was holding

the tampon between
my legs to the twitching
light in a Montana
bar when suddenly,
I screamed

"I fucking found $50!"
and took all my friends
out to dinner.

The red steak, the red
cheeks, red walls

of the bar, the red of
memory, red merriment,
red marry me, you
blurry monopoly.

Mother Money!

I was antidepressing,
having run out
of better drugs. (More
quarantine, more

problems.) The nocturnes

displaced strong
sentiments
in favor of a glistening flat
line.
I saw that poodle again
today sticking his
head out of
the garnet car. Poodle,
you're the winner
of the century!

Your statements have an
air of truth, Madame, so
please join us at the table.

The ceremony is about to
begin. It involves peonies,
the ambiance of a light
rain, the mourners (of
course), and a rare
appearance of a cherished
singer from the Old
World.

We would like you to
remember this is not
entertainment, but it is
acceptable to clap

softly or smile gently
when the table deems it
appropriate. I realize you
are morose today.

Maybe you have lost your
lover or maybe
you are deep in the
memory of our origin.

Let me tell you a secret:
Ours is a lost country.
Let it go for an hour

or two. Let the song
become your anchor or
vehicle.

We can't even die,
chained to our
subjectivity.
(Therefore, hell is *not*
other people, as one
might think, but rather . . .)

*Playwright gestures to
the audience.*

Did he accuse you of
ghosting him or did you
run for greener

pastures, other turbines,
other ramifications? Alas,
no, the issue's inside

the factory's time-
stamped algo/rhythm
ergo legacy of pre-
packaged diet
food and diarrhea
medication.

Vehemently opposed to
looters, the mob
sent out their moralizing
tweets. Personally,

I thought Target never
looked so good
wearing a disheveled
outfit or empty shelves,

smashed cash registers,
and a blaring (yet
useless) alarm. When
Auto-

Zone went up in flames, I
thought,
eh, let it rip. Oh Lysol-
sprayed

billionaire surfaces,
carapaces
of the national guard—
there is,

in reality, not much here
to keep.

Living with sickness is
difficult.
Mental exhaustion is real
and can't

easily be summed up
or disclosed. The desire
for a fine
narrative that comes to
the house like
a box from Amazon
you think will give you
COVID-19.
It won't.
Yours is a different
disease.

My love
slept through the winter.
What a great
spirit she was!

My love slept through
the fall
and summer! And when
she finally

emerged from her
somnolence, we
walked for miles and miles

and tried to recall
our life stories
before the conquering.

How will we go on?
The cornerstone of lust,
guilt, betrayal, animosity
arrives in the form
of missing people.

The town long deserted
has a ring of fangs
around the statuette.
Once they called this
place a precious fable.

She grows suspicious
of this community. They
exchanged the ones
she loved for farmland

and then exchanged
the farmland for
coffees implemented by
the millions.

*We hope you like how it
tastes.* It splashes
on her work pants, she
swerves into the next
lane, hits a pole.
Well, today's fucked.

But her books tell her
to notice, to *really
notice* harbingers—
ladybugs collecting in the
garage, a phone thrown
out the car window, a
trapezoidal dress glowing
white in the closet.

Don't harm yourself.
But if you must harm
yourself, let it be the least
harmful of harms.

Don't betray your
weakness or the jux-
tapositions of your
humors

or delights since the sun
goes on ravishing
even in the darkest
corners of the old house

where you sit on a chair
and pull a blanket
above your knees and
think about the long

night you underwent,
the mundane calamities
of remorse,
bewilderment

where you hurled your
body recklessly
into the dust. What came
out was smashed

(not uncharismatic) but
still. Now that you
are here, what is left?
What will you do
with the long, smoky
afternoon?

"Stay safe." But what if
that isn't paradoxical
enough for me? What if
I bring you a box

of goodies during these
bad times, sneak
past the barriers of faith
and longing,

just to see your pretty
(albeit confused) face
emerging from the freshly
painted barricades?

My tendons are sore from
running away.
Are yours? State violence,
harassment, bleeding out

the public hole, the core
cored and a corrugated
cord around a corroded
kiss until it was nothing

but a corpse. Who said
that every poem, in the
end, has a corpse
at its center?
Someone

or something uncanny
undoes
the symphony: could that
be the leitmotif

of this perverse
chronology?

"Why are you so chipper?
Did they burn
down another police
station or something?"

Do you know how long it
took me to pick
out the fake gold necklace
for the Zoom

interview? And now it's
all tangled because
I gave it to my kid.
Didn't even get the job!

"Hey buddy, where'd you
hide my cigarettes? Stop
being so holier-than-thou

and let me smoke in
oblivion. After all, it's
the end of the world."

"Hey, buddy. Oh wait,
you're my husband."

Forget Hey. Let's go
with Dear.

Dear stunning
Romanian poet.

Dear chronicle.

Dear ability to see
things I don't want

to see.
Dear anything.

Dear horses on fire in my
dream last night.

Planting a Loquat Tree   During the Worst Week   Of the Pandemic

FRIDAY:

Is it time to dig the hole?
Bury one and a half times
as—saying "goodbye" on
the i—"I don't even like
loquats." "Sand, if you
plant it there, it's going
to grow in-
to the electric—."

Dawn sky backlit by
brilliant pinks, deflated
Shamu's nose points into the
wooden fence, emergency
author—
the will of the—
later in the day—
overcharged
for organic—
take to customer—.

Carrie called, said
"the bag is on the door"—.
You really have to step
out of your—a shell
is a way to hear the sea,
the kids collected waves
and put them in a bowl.
Is it time to dig the hole?

THURSDAY:

I remember you said,
"we die surrounded,"
not alone (my fear).
Your wife shot
herself in the backyard.
I remember another
thing. You said, "why
didn't you drive back
to me, if you wanted to—?"

Open the medicine
cabinet. Why'd I keep
all the pills
that failed and failed?

Sky: cauldron cortical fog.
Wide-eyed tree. No
one's awake. Should
have sent you the—
I should have—.

MONDAY:

Three months'
supply of name-
brand antidepressants
costs $5,000. I shall
hitherto refer to
your every move
as the 1% of
brain chemistry—
disturb the root ball.

Cross section of thought.
Heavy cold shovel.
Deep cysts formed
on my—. You're allergic
to—neurotransmitters
refused to grow into
the electric—place
root ball gently
into hole.

I typed *dig
deeper* on my student's
paper about his two-
month rise to TikTok
stardom. Click on
a square, his body's
mosaic centimeter.
His muscular arm
twitches, glitches
over pixels of
Caribbean pool water.

WEDNESDAY:

You read my poetry
out loud to
your—. Remember
the way we gazed
at each
other full of—
full of—
at that house
party in Chicago?
I stormed through
the door, the decade.
Never followed.

I wrote back. Told
myself if I survived my
childhood I wouldn't
complain about—watched
a nurse named Sandra
on TV get injected
with the first vaccine.

Frost. It didn't
have to be like—
What? This?
Should have pulled
the bed-
sheet over
the thatched leaves.
Your eyes make me—.

SUNDAY:

Four times a day
drive past the spot
where the truck hit
the 14-year-old
girl and didn't—.

If I put roses
where the tree was
in this poem, will
I be forgiven?

Beeping of ICU
machines. 89% capacity
today. Stimulus checks.
Mindfulness group.
If you plant a—

Seed? Bone? Oh let
the little girl who lives
down the street come
over to play Scrabble
with my daughter.

Four times today
the girl told my daughter
she is getting a pony
for Christmas (a lie),
but I laughed. Russian
roulette—nucleocapsid,
tegument, genome,
envelope, in
these particles
of virus.

TUESDAY:

Looked at one
  way: Tropical
Cottages is
a dump. Looked at
  another: island
wind's azure-
  pink lips, hypoxic,
and palms sick,
  loaded with—unplug
the dripping air
conditioner, hear
song, liquor, squawking.

Man slumped
  over tiki bar 7 a.m.
while another man
gently sweeps a surgical
  mask and feather
into a pile on white
  bricks. I'll swallow
the sea today
  with my body.

Drove south south south
south. Woke at
  southernmost point
of continental US,
where a man rips off
his blue mask, takes
a swig of dried palm
leaf rum, says,
"I don't believe in
anything or anyone."

SATURDAY:

Ruche pattern
of light as I strolled
 through the rare
palm tree exhibit,
snakeskin palm,
paint peeling from
 the raw rhombuses
of sun on wood.
 Ruche honeycombs
as rays met a *window
 palm*, chlorophyll
on hand-
 written words . . .
careful, bee crossing.

Was supposed to be
 in Reykjavik, instead
tripped down a lime-
stone hill, bloody
knee, look behind
 me, a poised iguana
on a concrete slab

sunning its dorsal
 crest. Florida
Fish and Wildlife
 says if you see one,
kill it. If it shows up, kill it.
 Pest. Invasive. Kill it any-
 where. Kill kill
 tiki bar kill.

The fisherman looked
at me with such desire,
but stepped back from—

California orders
5,000 additional body
bags. Would some-
one I love—?

Took a photo of an
anhinga paddling north
toward the Atlantic.

The host in my mind-
fulness group asked for
a volunteer to read
the next paragraph.

"Some seeds die,"
I said, then
muted myself.

As in Leaving

One minke whale
was suspended
by six helicopters
above the fiery
caldera. They had
to please the gods,
so they sedated
its body that was
the size of
a school bus
and started
the procession.

The children
wore gas masks
and climbed the rocky
gradient without
their parents.
They had waited for
the new moon
when the sky
was clear
as a teardrop.

A brother and sister
huddled on the obsidian
slope holding hands.
The brother asked
his sister if she
was cold. She told
him that she wasn't
a baby and to let go
of her hand. Then
she kneeled down,
kicked off her red
clogs, and put
some dull ice in
her mouth.

The sister pointed up.
She could see the whale's
fins flapping
in the snowy air.

The Pyroclastic

Probably the wet
kaleidoscopes pointed
"out there" . . .

or maybe, Arnkatla, you
recall the grimoire
tucked neatly in a drawer

that smells of cedar-
wood and pipe smoke.

A little bit of this,

a little bit of that.

"Do you have any
powder?" the woman
with the rubber gloves
asks, pointing
to the stratosphere.

"In fact, I may,"
you answer, dumping
the contents of your
purse onto
the conveyor belt.

But there's more
to say about
the dormant
geyser—that it used
to blow 500 shillings
into the afternoon
chill every eight
minutes. One day,
a villager craned
his neck and peered
inside the hole.

"Nothing!" he shouted
triumphantly.

Strokkur chuckled.

Volcano

Our jet descended
through the alto-
cumulus cloud

bank and the metal
around us shook.

I took
a pill,

read a spell
from that igneous isle
we were leaving:

Inscribe this on a fox pelt
and color with blood from
your right ring-
finger and you will
not be haunted

by ghosts. The monitor
on the seat read
Happy Valley
Goose Bay.

I gulped.

The metal trembled,
trembled.

I choked on
the chalky sedative.

I grabbed
my husband's arm.

That's when they
heard the moaning,
splashing, and loud
yawn of the great
god the villagers
were trying
to please. By
then, most
of the children
had started
to descend the side
of the volcano.

"Mother would like
us to pick some artic
poppies and bring them
back to the cabin.
Tonight, she
is going to make
us stew," the sister said.
The brother nodded.

They gathered
as many white
flowers as they
could as they climbed
down. For a moment
the sister turned
back to look
at the caldera.
She could see
the minke
whale waving
from the top
and smiling at her.

I think we know
    what the son did.

Ah, mythology.
He had waited
    a long time for the death
of his father.
It was his turn
to destroy paradise.

The Future

Viruses disrupt
the market, distribute
packets of genetic
engulfment as
compressed cores
of time slowly widen
the orchids in the dim
ratios of survival.

Nonetheless, you wake up
in love but it's Frank-
ensteining together
a feather, velvet
mask, and shivering violet
hoping they become
the hotel room where
slanted angles of sun-
light reconfigure your
neurons so you can't eat,
sleep, or think of
anything.

Follow the dendrite
path of tree limbs
to their electric source—
the water between bodies
bursts with debris—DNA
fragments, misshapen
cells. I stared down
the ghost where it hurt
most—straight beyond
the ribs. I read the dead
poet's poems, gulped
in her pupils. I let
the house fall, couldn't
clean up the coffee
grounds or pick up
my tulip, satin robe
that rippled like a red
puddle on the cool,
wooden floorboards.

Is No Longer

Maybe we will go
to the mountains.

A philosophical
treaty of the ladder.

An editor asked what
I meant by *negation*.

The phonemes
of a Tuesday afternoon.

Beautiful creature,
I loved seeing

you, if even for
ten minutes in a year.

The corpus
that exceeds

the boundaries
of the book. A book

that exceeds
the silly idea of

making darkness
my only screen.

What It Was

Plunged into your cell
structures. To belong
inside you
 (but not to you)—

as one might belong
 inside the river-
stone's light you
mistake for ghostliness—.

(Text bad pictures
 of the daymoon
to any friend
 who will look.)

Outside, the Gulf doesn't
 know or care about
the National Guard
 surrounding
the New York suburb.

Inside, omens rupture
the surface as thunder
 makes the cup's juice
convulse. I knew

you would break
plans. Take a sip.
 Ugh grape. Spit it out
like medicine.

"I hope the day isn't
hollow," I said.

"Oh, it will be,"
you responded.

Your Eyes

A very thin girl
prone to melancholia
became a very thin
middle-aged woman
prone to melancholia
but she was nonetheless
loved. At first maybe
for her beauty
but eventually people
caught on to her tendency
to differentiate between
her failed mourning
and the potted palm
tree that looked
like the 19th century,
a pigment haunted
by chlorophyll, time
out of joint, yet
radiant. "I thought,"
she said, "the gradient
faced the grave
and I couldn't be
stopped like a train
jutting from the engraved
iris and ending in already
agreed upon cultural
production." Successful,
sure. Jubilant, no
doubt. Incantatory,
perhaps. But was it
anything worth
knowing? I have
seen it before, felt
it, heard it, known
it. It was the suf-
fering of the crowd,
the wheezing that she
internalized, oh how
they loved her
because she was
the memory of those
very few who had

Resemble

The truth is I wanted
to stay anonymous
yet I did not
receive enough FitPoints
from my phone to
give me a gold
medal today while
the deer click-clacked
up Mount Shasta Road
drinking the blue-
green algae, tripping
on one another, on fire,
on the choir of tainted
salamanders, on
the Gemini moon,
as they climbed the maze
of neural pathways
of valve and daze,
and maybe you
don't believe in true
love because it
isn't a distinct
enough transaction,
each movement, im-
pulse, sway
monetizing the day
of labor, retreat
from labor; it is
Saturday 11:55 p.m.
and I'm here to
tell you the deer
were authentic
troubadours and may-
be so were we,
just for a few
minutes crushed
between the cinder
blocks on the one-
way street, so
many times I meant
to call you but
troubles are very

Mine

"Nostalgia seduces
rather than convinces."
Perhaps, Svetlana,
perhaps. I saw a picture of
the beige L.A. apartment
where your first
inner experience of time
was dealt like a bad
hand of cards. The floor
of the casino
went wild, black
and red, seeing stars
that bled, and you
turned toward
withered expectation
as a concept to fulfill.
I noticed "the weird
artifice of my personality"
blaring from a boom
box on someone's
shoulder who was roller-
blading down
the amorphous
boardwalk. It was
like I had heard
the songs before,
even the songs
I knew I didn't
know. The past
reduced me to
an animal crushed
into a ball on
the shag carpet
and I was sentenced
to repeat the lyrics
the same way
my sworn enemy
had called my work
violent as her
bleached hair.
It is folly
to be ashamed

resisted turning
empathy into timed
protocols, or van-
ishing points woven
on the unreliable
horizon and thus
her flesh was the trace
of something crisp,
enhanced, alien
like the shock
of a dead body
returned in an ochre
dream, the erotic
tripling of water,
lust, and tree.
It was a day like no
other, clocks hanging
off ghosts, the jumbled
messiah of notes,
refusal, and the ash-
throated flycatcher
that just flew away.
Where had the bird
gone? Into the burned
gyre, she reckoned.
She turned around
and around and around
for the possibility
of growth.

private things
and sentimentality
is jealousy, the somber
roses. How hard
could it be to say
goodbye? Scrubbing
my face with dirt.
Am I ready? Goodbye,
morally speaking.
The abolition of
the family, the grotesque
forms of misery
and abuse, you grow
too accustomed
to even push
back against
the way you
pushed me through
the doors of the 7-
Eleven, albeit lovingly.
I have always been
humiliatingly
introverted, sur-
rounded by books,
deathly afraid,
and maybe this
alone (god
I hope so) resembles
something important.

of desire, I told
myself, but it
is also folly
to follow it.
Today is not
the today of decades
ago and no one
has a boom box
on their shoulder.
It was a nice spring
and the bright earth
was climbing to
my ankles in water
and weeds. The trees
were happy because
it rained and the birds
were happy because it
rained, and I was happy
because you got
away from the self-
surveillance mechanism
of our times. I saw you
running into (I'm not
sure) the same song
playing from decades
ago, but when I looked
at the sky I saw you
again: a gray, meteoro-
logical, swirling vacuity.

Poem   *With Three Lines*   *By Gustaf Sobin*

No hills left
to inhale.

What was only
true of your shiny, happy

century. We have twisted
the erotic like a rag

in antiseptic, our hands
chapped—air no

longer an orifice—
    a liability.

Progressing through
the political landscape

sprayed with pesticide,
we grazed as crazed

animals inhaling fumes.

Who's there?
The airstream.

*And why did you bother
coming today?*

We want   mostly
   to touch   each other
where sunlight burns
through glass
    turning us
    into   refracted,
watery   images
of poisonous
fungi   and lust.

[Ramming your body
into mine, just the quick-
ening of text messages
where the claimant
says, *this is a life.*]
[And it is. Somewhat]
[full of various
catastrophes] [lapping
the edge of an old
lake of algae. We want]
[mostly to fuck and
dangle from ancient
arches. We want mostly
to bicycle to the bakery
and bring back
a warm baguette
for our lovers.] [We want
mostly to careen
into the city and breathe
air without a mask]
[between the lips and
your body—hot,
awkward, and
painful. The Whole]
[Foods orchids re-
bloomed. How I waited
patiently (9 months).
By] [then they had
shut down entire]
[nations—eyes lacquered
thick with the virus
as other pathogens
rose like ghosts]
[from the snow melt.
The pressure pushed]
[my heart pushed
to one side, a force
stronger] [than
angst ramming
your body into]
[mine became] [the
microscopic telos
of these scorpion days.]

Tick

Debt-
scorched,
zombie-
bitten, gorging on
chunks of raw
data. Knows
you're mined.
Knows your move-
ments. Knows
you're meat before
the neurons fire.
Incumbent and in per-
petuity. Tu-
ition land-
scape. You're Fired!
Reads minds, i.e.,
the hour. Hoards
your longing.
Gives it back
in sunset-colored
smoke. Can't
stop watching.
Can't function.
Can't climax.
Can't cope. Poured
lava on the dope
face. It took
25 minutes
to scope the crowd
for a 2 second shot
of plasma booze.
My features buzz.
I fragment. I joke,
wire to the nook bespoke.
A school shoot-
ing sprouted
inside the nest
of the magnanimous
tree of life's got
energetic nodes.
Take, for example,
my childhood home

Tock

It felt good to cancel
my Audible subscription.
Couldn't return to
the plastic inside
my trachea. I said
don't text me, in-
stead let me feel
the contours of the awk-
ward pauses in your
waking voice.
"How's your job?"
"Kind of dead."
"How are the dead?"
"Kind of a job."
Remember when people
said not to write
about birds (too
feminine, boring etc.),
but imagine having
to navigate wind
turbines, the wired
suburbs? Dome
of forensic hives hid-
den in the gold-leaf
of the tonal center
like a pierced tongue.
Everyone has become
a very nice producer
of toxicology reports,
said a man named
Yung Shrimp. On his left
side an owl was screaming
and on his right side a shoe
was tying a shoe.
5G death knell
melodiously sublime
Galaxy Golden, Max-
west, MegaFon,
Caterpillar, Wellcom
pour into the intricate
fractal. You are quite
welcome and from

Cryptic

Intimately aware
in my glorious flesh
that all along
the future was just
bad hotel art
needlessly bolted
to the puce wall,
for no one was
going to steal
that painting
of the bridge's end.
Posts where the modernist
manifestos began
to unfold in in-
crements and you
pulled the sheet
over your head
and said, "talk to me,
tell me a story, say
anything and I will
resume my desperation
in the morning."
I turned off the lights
and the bridge
collapsed like a mid-
20th century public
works project.
I will smoke
outside this dive
bar, dim the electronic
night and try not
to be whimsical or
indefatigably bright.
I'm sorry I failed
you when you had
a breakdown and went
to jail. I should have
been more resolute.
My imagination mu-
tating, internalizing
disgust, an ache
turns to a story of

replaced by a bur-
geoning product, the center
of which is the con-
tiguity of my crooked
error. Swarm
of drones. About
the bleached arbor,
the pretty one
imitated the nature
of a scope. Posed
by the big bang.
Was asked not to
touch the rocks. She
thought the continuous
present was the worst
cipher for she could
no longer consider
specific emotions.
Overheard: "Because
people want to live
vicariously. Travel stuff
is good. You should start
capitalizing on that.
Put it in the forefront.
Have you heard
of a digital middleman?
There are other people
who are digital nomads.
You can turn everything
into a lifestyle." Or a net-
worked wrecking crew.

the wolf clan meaning
you're a pairing of eights
sprung from the relative
keys of water, the figure
turned over and push-
ing back against
the modes of pro-
duction was a bad
strategy for beauty
rushed in like a swollen
painting of a river
beneath the singed
hunter's moon
we counted the flocks
of debtors, payments
and lost checks, you
who are generating
batches of peripheral
blood, facial analysis
upon entering one's own
soul, urine, bile, typed,
transcribed in the in-
ordinate by an artificial
hum in the night's riverine
air, the places where
we went, the places
submerged in salty
digits, the pelicans carving
their flight paths through
fine-tuned hair analysis
and chilly fingerprints.

sex workers, low-
wage employees,
sea foam, velvet
and hypodermic smoke
that degenerates like
phantoms doomed
to exacerbate old
wounds. Take me
to the corridors where
cops troll every
conceivable footfall in
their crinoline capes
and waist-high
jargon. Handing
some psychotropic
plants to a friend,
some heirloom
tomatoes, goat
cheese, an air
purifier, six bad
masks, the image
of the arctic
alphanumeric
disaster-spoiled
analogue of fiber-
optic love, an
animal seeking
the inside of Beirut
or London for there
is no us . . . *is there?* . . .
to map the melt.

Dollar

It is a very lonely
experience to be so
full of words. Gilded
things help, but
not much.

In the ceramic
room glazed like the face
of an Etruscan queen,
I have my supply of

plants, drugs, glass jar
of watermelon
seeds—possibilities.
Cold Florida day

without the roll
of thunder just this receipt
paper the Dollar Tree
cashier handed to me—

so many stories emanate
like synapses of fog
on the man-made
lake unfurling

where the heron
becomes neurons
on the roll as the scroll
transforms some

artifact to unearth
—scarab painted
against the iridescent
Atlantic on fire—.

"Oh go ahead and take
it!" the cashier said
staring right into the
security cameras. I shoved

the roll into my purse.
Shampoo. Metal

Tree

Sunrise 7:05 a.m.
(November) astro-
nomical twilight 5:
42 a.m. total 57 mins
to squeeze in
a reverie or two be-
fore the radio
commentator tells
us the vaccine's
consistency is
like melted chocolate,
needs to be kept
at −80 degrees C
run on deep
freezers ringing
up items in signals
and waves she
threw a can of
corn into the cart
a migraine in the
hurricane rush out
of the form it
came from nowhere
like pulling a gift out
of a bag and
the child has learned
to pretend to
like the doll
with its plastic
hair no corn silk
here and if you
push a button
she will sing
an American hymn
"We can dye
her hair purple"
I suggest in November's
hopeful glare
and in comes the email
to tell me I didn't win
a fellowship but look,
you don't get to
steal all my

Poiesis

For death write *life-
robbery*, for raven,
swan of blood. Call

air *a vulture path*.
Refer to the coast
as the outlying sanctuary

of the sea rib. Bad
poetry is *the dung
of the ancient eagle*.

A mountain should
hitherto be called
the place where wolves

drift or *the land
of mountain cats* whose
paws are ice-crackling
prints crossing wilderness

while *the skull-pickers*
(vultures) soar above
as *the breaker
of trees* (wind) howls

and fills *the cup-liquid
of the undead* (poetry)
with tampons, nail polish,

bras; language is a branch
that breaks cryptic from
deific so I must ruin,

unearth, unscramble
words, for the gods
delight in concealment.

I lived in the house
of sand and seaweed.
I made turkey with

chestnut stuffing,
roasted potatoes

frog garden decoration,
toothpaste, hair ties.

When my kids
were little and I had no
money, I would stroll
in the store and declare

"you can buy anything
you want!"
That's how kids get
the idea they can be

president. Now, it's Chris
who said "you have to put
that receipt paper into your
book." I guess I was

going to leave it out, let
the reader feel the debris,
detriment, lyric deviations
from materiality but now,

come to think of it, it's
time to confess to reality.
Oh right, about
all that anguish. No

sense in surrounding
it. Try holding its hand
and going for a walk to
the poisoned pond.

The poodle is overjoyed,
pushes her wet nose out
the front door. My
daughter says she

downloaded an app
that can translate dog to
English. Can you sit still
among these ruins?

Now Calypso's kicking
the air, whimpering but,

attention, you
don't get to squeeze
the fresh morning
out of my lungs yet
and fill them
with data
particles, ads
propaganda,
disappointment sun-
rise on March 15
2019 was 7:30 a.m.
Mark your calendars
because I bought a
red silk robe and I'm
ready to levitate over
the lake big toes skimming
the daydream's
cracked sounds
Leeches, dead people,
snakes, coffins, worms
and bats—those are
the only things women
in Freud's texts
dream of but really it's
only what *he* decided
to fixate on—pond
full of toads I think
when she was in
the garden she didn't have
the "oppressive thoughts"
he imagined her
to have but instead
she was fucking
with him when she
said, "the dead
man was eating me out"
Interpret that as
a theory of the private,
as she boarded
the posh 747, DC-
10, DC-9, -8, backward
in time they served
steak, ice cream bright
jade room, brighter
in altitude the spirit

with caramel, saffron.

In the morning, I baked
bread. Evening, I sat
at a small table in a room

entirely composed of
cobalt glass, and I took
to my lips that drink

of the undead and my cup
was cracked and my lips
were also cracked,

and I settled into these
unclaimed stories
with a bowl of sticky

toffee pudding, Double
Happiness cigarettes,
words, lots of them,

wielded, unscrolled, wove
while the laughter of my
children shook the glass

and seeds in the garden
erupted from black soil,
corpses from tulips.

De scinderatio fonorum.
My fingers pulsated.
I'm the one who cuts up

harmonies, descends
scales, I'm the one who
obliterates metaphor,

replaces it with the script
of forest's leaves making
blankets under drones

inside the ocean, terror
place, my kids
downloaded, shelved,

overall, a satisfied
creature, dreaming, below
the iceberg of dreams.

hello I'm so sorry
paper that can't grow any
longer, can't unroll,
paper that can't go on
longer, can't unroll,
or ring up any new
characters, ideas, fingers,
beep beep the story
halts I look through
plate glass, light the tip
of the frankincense
for now it is spring
If I have indulged too
much in signs
If I have gone too far
If the sonic disturbances
were too elongated
mea culpa
If I subtracted
mea culpa
If my gestures
If my voice

consciousness in wind
shear and now have
turned to fighting over

an electronic keyboard
"the most important thing
in the house right now

is that your mom is
writing a poem," I hear
said, shrill scream, open

the blue doors, pass
through discordant glass,
notes fade, a light rain,

banging of a bedroom
door, scroll for the right
word "terror," no already

used that one so I must
intervene, "can't
you just share

the keyboard?"
Are they still fighting?
But I'm just one mind

in the ether with
all the other minds

and I'm dead too
on the receipt paper
with pencils, Lysol,

a can opener. Call it
fire waves, scroll on,
call it *the swallower*

of the sky, or *the high
flickering flame
of the world's hall*,

or *the bright roof
of the storm*.

Hold!

I sat   in the orbis,
in the docket of my debt.
The truth is, I wanted to
remain   unknown.
Tell us about your work.
No.   No.   No.
Eyewall   sustained
by intensities, eyewall
drinking   the blue-
green algae (scum
on a song)   listened to
    over and
over. *Tell us about*
your work.
    Oh.   It is real.
(That's why   it is
    so synaptic.)
The salesgirl pulled
at my jewelry.
"You like circles,"
she said, "gold ones."

Said the Hand

Climate change
    has totally fucked with
ancient spells. We just
    can't find
ingredients. Where can
you find   a lion cub
to slaughter   with a
    bronze   dagger? How
are you   supposed   to
    wash its   small heart
with wine   for three
years to possess   the one
you love?   Overturn
    the ruin—the underside
smells of   myrrh, mid-
    summer, underworld:
You like gold ones.

Said the Money

Xi Jinping pours
200 billion
units into the besieged
firmament, into
the azure orbis
of frost and fog.
Supply chain com-
ponents of the vast
solid dome
are man-
ufactured in
Turkey, Czech
Republic, and Mont-
gomery, Alabama.
But instead of a one-
click purchase,
you sit quietly
looking at books
while everyone
is saturated with
the flickering. You
wrap yourself in
text. The gold
circles of crypto
were lonely
without you,
but you followed
your finger
down the old-
fashioned page.
Sirius, you read,
was called
the scorching
done by Loki.

To Take a Lover   In the Intricately Woven   Kaleidoscope

Intricately woven
  but very soft,
the suds
  of catastrophe,
lethargic and hung-
  over like the eucalyptus
trees in September,
  October, gently peeling
away yet none-
  theless charismatic.
    I was strangely
      intrigued by
poetrylover-
    inthesky who said
    and I quote . . . would
      look much better
    if you didn't post your
      obvious tit shots,
    whore . . . and I quote
      quote quote sleeping
    in the nude, making
  myself revisit
the plastic over the air
vent or the sluice where
  dreams grind
down the skeleton.
  Who was she he or they
and how was it that
  one could flee into
the beautiful, anonymous
  epithet of the breezeway?
    Maybe he thought
      I loved him.
    No, that is absurd.
      Maybe she thought
    I loved her.
      It cannot be.
    The mediocre book
      floats before me,
    and when I try to pull
      it to my chest, it
    evaporates.
    But I insist!
      Something must
      stay here, some-
    thing con-
      crete and
    absolvable.

To take a lover
  in winter
when it is just
  as hot as summer
these days which is
  to say the abey-
ance slipped
  deep into nocturne
fractals transitioning
  the digital stream
to the wet body.
  I have asked
far too much
  of you and now
the correspondences
  we once cherished
have been left
  in the gulch
to simmer and dis-
  close, dis-
close, disclose.

In the kaleidoscope
  of walnut trees,
    why did
  I allow myself to
    meet you just
      to feel more lonely
afterward? Face
reality and all
  of its circuitry—
    doomed to make
      the same er-
        otic mistakes.

Dear Anselm,

I was thinking of
the squares or grids
or grids within grids
or maybe thought
patterns cross-
listed as codes
the way we are
supposed to create
some analogue
version of the self
with language and
a couple of clouds thrown
in the mix since
this is a landscape
made from natural
light and you are
a tree now. Maybe
it is stupid to
walk through
art so quickly
probably only looking
for a place to charge
my phone which
is sick and dying
and full of photos
of art like this
one painting made
by Alice Neel
of an adult human
holding a baby
human or maybe
the baby is holding
the adult human
in a suit and tie
the way labor
is reproduced back
and forth
unconsciously
and they look at you
like you're

Feeling mostly dismay
or a variety of symp-
toms, not sure
what time it is. Early.
Oh yeah hosting
a poet today. Drove him
around South Georgia
all day. Poet wrote
of small towns in
the Midwest. I write
about plutocracy,
stupidly drank
too much coffee,
arose like the golden
phoenix. Learned of
a Marxism con-
ference going
on. Not invited (duh).
Why is this day so
long, almost un-
bearable but the poet
shouted the word
"DINGBAT!" at
lunch which was . . . er . . .
bizarre. I would read
in a pizza parlor
turned funerary
debris as I am always
rising from the dead
weight, belatedly, sure,
but who hasn't
been a symbol
crushed for its raw
material and collected
in an urn? I hope
the drive home is
hazy and dotted
with poplars. I hope
it is only one
version of a cheap

Welcome back!
Today, my kitchen almost
caught on fire because
I spilled rice all over
the burners
and the expensive
people fired half
the faculty
at the university
where I teach so more
than likely the ship is
going under. I excused
myself from the family
to write something
for a few minutes
(this). Well, truth
be told, I may be
a little drunk
and autofill already
knows what my poem
will say which isn't freaky
as much as it is suicidal
and yet I saw the moon
today and it was mighty,
mighty pretty,
and I managed to clean
the house and even
managed to wrap some
cookies in napkins to
bring to my kids but now
I am wandering off
as I am prone to do . . .
I am happy about your
daughter's bat mitzvah.
You know, that's a lot
of fucking work!
Learning a new language
etc. My son will be in
middle school
in 6 months. He has

supposed to be
surprised or whimsical.
My mood right now
is polylingual
and will probably
disappear shortly
into the intrepid
street thrown from
one supremely
constructed box to
another like this
homeless man
with the backdrop
of a fashion model
in neon feathers
eating an orange
but her one-
dimensional image
can't live naked
with splendor.
Now we are
in the plastic
tunnel of air
that keeps the plane
airborne and
there's a call
for a doctor because
there is always someone
who is going to
pass out up here.
Well, wake up!
The truth is
I probably won't
mail your MoMA
card back to you
since I am so
lazy about making
it to the post office
and always promise
everyone I'll go
but end up gutted or
strangely embarrassed
crossing the street
with no
obvious corrective.

painting and that
there will be others,
and I hope the drive
takes a really long
time. I mean
a really long time
to get to the original.

terrible stage fright
but wrote a speech
for his class about
the world on fire—
the burned koalas
falling from eucalyptus
trees and all of that
and delivered it today.

Pastoral

Had sex in the national
park looking up through
the latticework of leaves,
touched Earth's watery
flesh, the skin of last
year, impenetrable
apparition, timescale
shift like finishing
The Norton Anthology
of English Literature
Volume
2. Which way
now? Marginalia?
Do you think it's criminal
to try to squeeze some
pleasure out of this
embalmed wasteland?
Walked to the middle
of the river, some
men hovering
around the birth-
place of toxic
masculinity like wasps
but really they seemed
more like graves,
ridiculous, knowing no
one would care about
their musculature
in fifty years.

It rained on and off
all night, the tent
warm and clean, my green
tennis shoes soaked
through (rookie error).
Caught hidden cameras
in the rocks.
Fined for public
indecency. Better to
arrest hummingbirds,
chipmunks, chunks

In the Minor

History's great tides.
The artist rises
in a sapphire room.
Something immaterial—
fluvial, eked out
of the shift between rain,
between rain. My voice
stems from a certain
amount of intellectual
experience punctuated by,
"see, it's Mr. Rabbit," my
daughter says and sure
enough the creature is
hiding under a bush
I've been trying to kill.
Note to self: write
2 hours a day, only 15
minutes of social
media, 1 hour
reading, check air
quality: *unhealthy* but
I will still go running
until my little lungs
get all sooty and wet,
laden with virus and
calamity, until they
wheeze vowels and cramp
up—pushed to extinction.
Saharan dust cloud
making its way across
the Atlantic
Ocean and I'd like to
prove to you that I still
have feelings, that I could
write long, jangling
essays about them, that
my body still wants
other bodies, that I still
want life despite
my numerous addictions
and abject failures!

Key

My phone is idiotic.
It tells me that my car
is parked at my house 15
feet away where I am
making my morning
coffee and looking at my
car. There is something
very sad about those 15
feet because I don't want
to be made aware of this,
yet I know it and I will
never stop knowing it.
If I decide to bake bread,
I will know the car is still
15 feet away. Inanimate
bulk of metal, you've
ruined my life by not
being the getaway car
you promised you
would be! I've wasted
years on these sorts
of equations and noting
the absurdity doesn't
do much to decrease
the sadness of pouring
oatmilk onto oatmeal
but I'm determined
to write an aria today,
demystify the polluted
air with homeless notes
the pitches of which are
strung together like
the way I used to gather
rent money, always
finding a few bucks under
the sofa cushions, or
maybe selling a poem and
losing the check that I got
for the poem I sold about
trying to pay rent
while dreaming of a little

of quartz
at the bottom
of the mossy pool!

In the morning, drove
by the upside-
down White House, (Las
Vegas of Tennessee),
a place to rent a machine
gun, a shack selling
moonshine of all kinds—
cherry, piña colada, one
blue as a beach towel—
and I pressed my hand
through some tiny
fissure right into
a past life, from which
only the most persistent
spirits escape.

Notebook: what I liked
about the disgraced poet
is that she did not
apologize. Shame: to
cover oneself. Dis-
grace: to deprive
of fortune. Fortune:
a goddess personifying
luck. Luck: perhaps
related to "lock," which
means a hole. I am
digging a hole
in the garden
with my bare hands.
This is where the loquat
will grow and grow.
Now I go to the shopping
mall to get my phone
unlocked. I am planting
bulbs in holes. I have un-
locked the garden.
This is my luck,
my shame, my dis-
grace, my cover, my hope.

gathering of poets
exchanging work for free
and now it is mid-
morning and the rabbit
has darted across
the front lawn
and I am picking up
the newspaper where I
have written a few things
about a poet I admire.
Here I am. I have
not moved
more than 15 feet.

The Only Cloud in the Sky

One thing—snowdrift
comes to mind.
So I am not holy. Rather the
inverse of the alphabet
mapped onto the painting,
dogwoods—I would
go with you to them.

Frightening twins of noon!
Omen mist stretched
to healthier hymns. Be-
reave my thin flesh, pin
my genome's nth point.
Tiptop gods of wild, woo me:
your gems outwit youth.

To Impress Me

Carpet of weeds, diadem.
Shore lifting chopped reeds
in sprays to torrents—
moss-colored fury.
Do you want to
gravitate toward my
onomatopoeias & currencies?

The firs weep, the firs
are fertile signs that
traverse in twos, in threes,
make codes for rooms, undo
wounds, drama, ravaged
data or diagrams. I touch
your righteous enormities.

With a Demoniacal Grandeur

Softly begging the landscape
inside my thwarted
miseries, my cryptic
dialectics. Sorry I can't be.
Go. No don't go
on that way, I said.
Credit card declined.

Gently letting the tenths
arrive, she died in winter,
skidded the secret mimicry of
ice symmetries, coinciding
with lyres, rioters. Your
hideaway awash. I awaited—
an addict encircled in red.

~~pin-~~
~~pointed a universal~~
~~fabric, a thick, sludge~~
~~matrix speeding up~~
~~slowing down~~
~~simultaneously~~
~~surrounding my tiny body~~
~~and I woke up almost~~
~~an improvisation~~
~~of limbs, yes, *that* gutted~~
~~so I lit some incense~~
~~and did a cheesy little~~
~~meditation prayer~~
~~maybe I just need~~
~~a cup of coffee this~~
~~morning scrolled~~
~~through family texts~~
~~*12,000 people very little*~~
~~*leg room, people were in*~~
~~*tears when she sang*~~
~~*the* Titanic *song*~~
~~*use Lysol Wipes*~~
~~*on the airplane even*~~
~~*the seatbelt*~~
~~*Sunny here so should*~~
~~*have no delays*~~
~~then walked down~~
~~the boardwalk *I can't*~~
~~*help it, I love it when*~~
~~*a cute boy likes my*~~
~~*profile pic,* all the cracks~~
~~of society opening~~
~~some fool politician~~
~~talking about "safety~~
~~nets," meanwhile virus~~
~~spreading in prisons~~
~~and if these bastards~~
~~buy all the coffee~~
~~I really might~~
~~become a homicidal~~

~~maniac, scroll, scroll,~~
~~scroll they were going on~~
~~and on about Celine in~~
~~Las Vegas and even . . .~~

~~Fuck it, no, the world~~
~~isn't going to end with~~
~~Celine singing from~~
~~history's sinking~~
~~boat, oh no, it won't—~~
~~gluts in the supply chain~~
~~spit out trembling hands~~
~~or the hands of~~
~~treacherous~~
~~thieves reselling basic~~
~~necessities. "We're~~
~~just hustlers." My sister~~
~~says they are just going to~~
~~let it rip like a dystopian~~
~~culling in the UK~~
~~no, it won't end~~
~~with Celine Dion because~~
~~it's not even raining today~~
~~and some of us have~~
~~learned how to make~~
~~homes on the surface of~~
~~the sun and we carry on~~
~~without burning~~
~~or rather, we have been~~
~~burning for so long that~~
~~what can put us out?~~

~~My only hope for the day~~
~~is that Trump gets the~~
~~coronavirus and I see~~
~~a pod of dolphins.~~

Update: both
happened.

The Flammagenitus Strophes

You pick me up late,
   a viscous outflow

from the volcanic ledge
of my thinking.

Me, in my duplex-hunger,
in my firestorm-astonished
dress, the pattern of crisp
   asphalt, the pattern,
   simple condensed

nuclei, against my dry
   lightning ache.

We drive through
polyhedronated structures

of sound and civic-
   minded lives,
   lives bearing fruit
   with no regard

for the termination-
   tables recently
made, vast ledgers

of waste, of debits,
of human trees.

Debris is my name, I say
   as we drive past

the decibels, the altostratusly
   hung steeples, *debris is*

my name I say, wind
streaming in fil-

aments, collecting

  in the gorge,
our mouths barely
   resonating.

It Was Raining in the French Concession

It was a thunderstorm.
Or smog. Or both.
All I know is
the particulates
glowed and hung
like ghosts in the post-
human twilight.
It was raining in
Shanghai, which
is the beginning
of a tragedy, joke,
or poem and there
were lanterns
all around Elevator
(the nightclub) and
the Russian girl (a DJ)
was talking about
something I couldn't
hear much. Oh she
was talking about
her podcast
which was about
what DJs do during
the day "when they're not
DJing" and on a screen
there was computerized
art that seemed
as if the air was not
the air as though you
felt that negation
was artificial
and turning.
I think you know
what I mean,
the way demons
turn to look
at you or churn out
some new cartography.

You talked about
"Mansion."
No, not "THE mansion."
There was no article.
"Do you want to know
about Mansion?"
I said, "not really."
I felt self-conscious
and distant
and thought about my
lover 15,000 miles away
and texted him that I
would visit him soon
and told my son
I would bring him
home a Chinese drone.
I wanted desperately
to hear something
harmonious but we were
inside the topography
of the information
of feeling. Your veins
were circuits and
so were mine.
"Teenagers all around
Shanghai go to
Mansion—losers,
the riffraff,
dropouts of all sorts,
they do drugs and things."
Of course they do, I thought.
I couldn't hear
anything else you said.
I do remember saying,
"but shouldn't they read
and plan a revolution?"
"They should read
more, I agree," you said
but it was too loud
to hear anything else.
Outside, a guy from

When I got back
to the hotel I thought
about the bees rising in
the black smoke from
Russia which was in
the poem by Han Bo my
friend translated as
the wind blew in the hotel
windows and the gridded
world unleashed
something like steel, teeth,
concrete, unto me.
The curtains were
drenched with my sweat
and all night I dreamed
about that atmosphere
of growth and capital,
the percentages
a cross between light and
agony, I dreamed so much
when I woke up there was
glass on the floor
and I cut my foot walking
to the bathroom
as I gulped in
the starched night
like a puffer fish.

The next afternoon
my friend and I walked
in the French concession.
We passed an old woman
selling paper replicas
of everything valuable
in this world. My friend
said, "you can buy
a paper mansion—you
burn it to honor your
ancestors." You can buy
a paper iPhone.

Corsica asked, "why
are you at Elevator?"
I said, "I do not know
why I'm at Elevator,"
and he drank and talked
about Corsica's Eternal
Forest and right then
I wanted the Eternal
Forest to hold me close
and later I read on the
Internet "Wildfires
sweep Europe as Lucifer
Heatwave makes its
way. . . ."
It must have been
a bad translation.

A paper Ferrari.
A paper jet.
A paper laptop.
As he said this, my friend
seemed to be pointing
to oblivion.
"She's got paper
everything."
A paper yacht.
"You can burn that."
You can buy a paper
elevator and burn it,
a paper elevator
to everyone
who came before you.

Double Happiness, or

At this P. F. Chang's
in the Detroit airport
playing Xmas music
surrounded by
baseball caps
I'm pretty sure someone
is eating a whole cabbage
and I'm carrying a drone
back from China
for my son
It's called
the Ghost Ranger

"Modernity

In two days, unbeknown
to me, right now,
drinking beer with
sports
people in this
aviation space,
that drone
will end up
caught in the backyard
pine tree
dead drone not
coming down

Means Contingency"

"Do what you do well,"
my student said
he is the former
poet laureate
of Sacramento so
I revolved or revolted
like the diamond
or the oracle spitting
out rhythms
of the selfsame
compartmental
space I tried to exude

Skate

What I want today
   is to roller-skate like
when Merleau-Ponty
   says, "the body is
our general medium
   for having a world,"
glide side by side
   the hyaline, celestial
beats. I push up
my bra orbs or
   rivulets in the sword-
like light fervor from
   the strobe dynasty
for everyone
knows this poem
is really a hole.

World

Acoustically not
   there like the back-
beat in Shanghai's
   electronic music scene.
Volt. Volt. Current.
   This sine or
synthesized coagulation
   my blood clot surface
called feelings or
   hysterics. In am-
plitude, in other-
   wise pyriform
tabulates. I was
   inside your octave
and you felt it
   say you felt it
I was inside
   the periodic bursts
of light called
   thermosphere.
Composite host,
   hold me close,
you're just a fucking
   baby or com-
bination of switches.
   Stole some shit
from CVS and
   I became Footage
Girl who always gets
   away with it. Phase
Shift—just drown
   in harmonic spec-
trums. Inverse the fre-
   quency for me.
   The key's
under telos's armpit.
   Hey, I love you,
cookie. Intuitive
   verbs fizzle in
precise quantities,
   I'm not a fucking
theorem though

Waveform

The wind blows
   ocean layers over
gravity, oscillation.
   I could hit you
now. We collapse
   on ourselves like
space. The cities
   we are from lean
forward, ask us
   to saunter into
their buildings
   or deteriorate,
break like people,
   like us. I could
kiss you now, but
it wouldn't be
   proper. I bought
some probiotics
   for my vagina.
They were expensive,
   surging in the blood,
deepwater motion
   no origin like
us, the cashier
   said she liked
my earrings. I said
   they are anchors
she said "oh"
   and I'm a ship
with a long, beautiful
   wavelength. I get
so turned on
   by water, the way
astronomical forces
   collide the internal
   weather you don't
even know how
   important that is
the inner weather
   but it's everything
you barely notice
until it's too late—

and even now I'm
just smoking
   a cigarette on
the sidewalk out-
   side the music
hoping it will
   come out and give
me my sweater.
   Integral thighs—wet
like conditions.
   It was raining when
I fell in love with
   all my mistakes.
Everything "behaves
   nicely," until you
begin to hemorrhage
   sound, everything
"behaves nicely"
until the derivatives
   bleat decay like glass
structures that atrophy
   in starlight. Give
me a light. Turn
   me around. It was
always the hole,
thinking, plotting,
   growling. Gladly,
you say and walk
   off. Go find your
identity, rep-
   licate your genome.
It won't be long
   until you're standing
in front of me again
   wondering how
   I knew you.

that was you, wasn't it,
   piled up,
periodic vacillation.
   Perturbed.
Can't you just?
   That was you.
Voice refracted.
   Can't you just?
Beige hallways.
   Can't you just?
Nondescript office space.
   Can't? Move on.
That's what people do.

Trashland

I'm not a great
lover I told
the senator &
he said that's okay
I'm not a great
politician. But
you won re-
election I said
& he said
that's because
I lie about every-
thing. Remember
when we first
met at the air
force base around
all those intelligence
officers & I said oh
yes I remember
the way you spread
cream cheese
on my bagel &
handed it to me
in the most
affectionate way.
That was, of course,
before you became
the Honorable
Senator, when you
were merely
a cog in the state
of things, & wasn't
I also a cog
in the state of things
with my insipid
anorexia, klepto-
mania, plaid
skirts & constantly
running away so it
wouldn't be surprising
that we would
continue to cling
to each other, life

Political

The walls
of the tropical
cottages were painted
pink & white
& a tabby cat sat
outside pawing trash
suspiciously.
In the room,
the senator opened
his briefcase & spilled
the contents out on
the bed: a receipt
from a Mexican place
in Echo Park, a small
snow globe with
a parrot in it that
said Jamaica.
I shook it
wildly. He laughed,
got naked, did
drugs. Then he said
the air-conditioning is
very loud so we
ripped it out
of the wall & I
would say we trashed
the hotel room
but the place
was already a dump.
After we made love,
we walked to the ocean
& he implored me
to throw my iPhone
into the tide because
no one should
know anything
about anything about
anything which was
almost a motto by now
tattooed into the very
depths of my being.
I shrugged.

Economy

A week later, having
returned to Tallahassee
from the Keys, I turned
on my lavender phone
with no contacts in it.
To be sure, it was a
barren place & isn't that
what the senator wanted,
no contacts? I opened
a browser & saw him
in a wooden hall
huddled under a desk
between chairs,
holding hands with
a woman. I zoomed
in to the point of contact
between his hand
& hers. They looked
scared to death.
I tapped & tapped.

Maybe it is cold-
hearted but I closed
my browser & thought
I'm sure he'll be fine.
He always is. Later
that night, I got drunk
& threw the phone into
my swimming pool.
It wouldn't sink.
Nothing does.
The next day, I went
outside & drank
coffee & gazed at
the rippling blue pool.
The phone began
to tremble violently.
Some nervous energy
overtook me
& I jumped in like I was
rescuing a baby.
The daymoon glittered

rafts, mirror
neurons of
a warped system.

Why not? It's not like
this thing doesn't
bring agony straight
to my fingertips.

Then he gave me
three new cellphones.
I said I really don't need
three new cellphones
but he said, my darling,
I insist, my gift to you.
I chose the lavender one
& said thanks. He pulled
a Norwegian passport
from his pocket. I opened
it & saw a picture
of myself at sixteen.
Where did you get
this I said & he said where
do you think & I said
I don't know anything
about anything &
he said that's exactly
where you got it
& put it into my purse.

in my hands.
I'm okay texted
the senator.
I was shivering.
The chlorinated day
had just begun.

An Equanimous Defense   Of the Exclamation   Point

Hi There.
My name is Karen
and I'm calling to
share some brief
words of encouragement
from the Bible
today. You may be on
a recorded line
for quality assurance.
Hang up. Now it's
an old friend
from Santa Cruz who
says a crew
from Hollywood
is going to remodel
his house for free,
then tells me a serial
killer murdered someone
there in the '70s.
"Aren't you afraid?"
"Dude, there's no soul,"
he said.
"I'd still be afraid."
"It was some drug
thing. LSD or whatever."
"I'd still be . . ." Who
has destroyed death
and brought
immortality to life?

Karen again.
The world is vast
and bleak.

My 8-year-old
has gotten into
the nasty habit
of saying she hates
me at least
once
a day.

Io is Latin
for "hooray." Medieval
copyists placed
an *Io*
at the end of
the sentence,
emphasizing joy.

Do you feel joy,
Karen?

At some point the *I*
was drawn over
the *o* and the ex-
clamation point
was born in the
strained opponens
pollicis of the monk
who may not
have wanted this
life looking out
the small triangular
window of
the monastery—
all he sees are
chestnut trees
and the moon
which he mistakes
for oh Sandra what
does he mistake it for?

It must have been
difficult, mixing
iron gall
from the twigs
of an apple oak
with acid to form
the blackest ink
so that he could write
by candlelight
in a language
not his own, in a city
not his own, in a world
he could barely recognize.

Why hello there.
It's Karen. I'm
reminding you
to be kind no matter. Why
hello there. It's Karen.
What. I see the world
is dipping you
into the mouth
of an active
volcano. I'm
reminding you. Why.
Hello there.
To be kind. I see
you have
developed a
hacking
cough. Hello.

Again. It's Karen. It's.

I see you have.

I don't like.

I'm reminding

you. I don't. No

matter.

Hello. There. The

world is. The

circumstance.

Choose. Hi. Kindness.

New

Medical staff signals
hulks of metal into
their own lanes
of sorrow. Drove
down down down.
"Turn off all the vents
in the house," the nurse
said. Made
love furiously
off the trail the day
before, our flesh
crushed in by the curved
silk of grasses.

Bed felt like a morgue,
but here, oh here,
I even loved the sharp
granite pressed into
my back, looking up
at loops of cloud,
crows. Rose.

Took photos
of the burned oaks,
all those alien formations
in that cold Eden.

Year's

I took a pill
even if it gave me horrible
acne because
I wanted to be normal.

Zodiacal visions
of ivy, wasps, lava
went gray
but the world was
the same—$600
deposit, trays of mac
and cheese left
outside my 8-year-old
daughter's door.

Sparrow flew
into the house; got
the broom, shooed
it out. "Do your thing,"
I told the bird, but it
was already gone.

"What day is it?"
my daughter coughed.

I couldn't answer.

Requiem

Great blue heron, mid-
flight over the COVID-
testing car line.

Do your eyes water?

How long between metaphors?

*How much does it take
to evaporate?*

Does the swab hurt?

Are you good at chess?

*Are there hills where you're
going?*
        A factory?

A school?

        A sea?

*Do you feel
the violet slipstream?*

Makeup

Fall into
  the fabrication
of the human
  face says
the palette
which operates
  as displacement.
These heels
are uncomfortable,
  but I like to tower
over sweat and drops
  of liquor. Ultraviolet
leggings, I felt

guided by pigment,
  the silver mothership
of the polar sea
  all-night-long-
lasting jumbo
  spray tan. You see,
it was the demands
  of the surface
that produced
  discordances,
the music, static
  drowning in adorables,
the smell of pleather
  and cigarettes.

Ointment

They rode
out to the docks
  where the world
stank of brackish cod.
He thought of his
  student who spoke
a language no one
  had ever heard of.
The student sat
  in class and nodded
yes, which meant
  he didn't know
what the hell
  was going on.

The trees
  are balms
and the balms
  are hidden.
The wind blew
  their hair
exquisite but
  she didn't say
much besides
  "look at the water,"
which was rippling
  faster, faster
as evening
  brushed across
the surface—swarms
  of brackets, the way

Pollen

What a strange elegy
that begins with
  a national coin
shortage and a family
  at the laundry mat
perplexed.
  They will find
another way.

Say you are walking
  to your car
and before you
  even get in, you
notice a thick
  film has built up
on the contraption.
  But why travel
  anywhere? These
days are rocks
  sinking to the bottom
of a beautiful
  brook full of fish
and sparkling moss.

What's the difference
  between veins
and arteries? Just
  a matter of direction
from the heart or to
  an opening in
the disco ball
  so now the grave
sings of oxygen,
  carbon dioxide.

you reach down
  for the water
when you're
  in a canoe
and let it flow
  across your
fingertips . . .
but maybe
  I should

Going from town
  to town, you turn
up the volume—
  Is that Supertramp?
and your left
  eyelid is twitching
and it seems
  there's a little
too much
  hair on the comb.
It must be the atmosphere
  full of crossbills, the flux
of iridescent energy.

"At the present moment,
  I care more about
Drosera than
  the origin of all
the species in the world,"
wrote Darwin. He poured
boiling water on
  their carnivorous
leaves, sprinkled
cinnamon, acid, sheep's
milk, inserted needles
  over and over into
them, took
  careful notes
morning and night
  wondering if
the sundews
  would die.

They did.

stop, deep
  calls to deep,
and propose
  instead of trying
to fix things, to
  gather a collection
of unlikely charms:
  worm snail shells,
caved-in sand dollars,
supremely wrought
lightning whelks, spotted
  slippers and you
have vanished into
ripples, and now

Once again
  the conifers
are loaded with cones
  and before you know
it, it's October
  but we are still
in the same mess
  watching screens.
She said her
  goal weight was
zero. I thought
  it was a mistake.
Someone said,
  "then you would
be dead"
  and she said,
"that's the point."

These experiments,
  this love affair with
torture (can you
  call it torture?), lasted
years and years.

it's just me, the broken
harbor with its
  injured birds, and I've
become the bearer
  of phosphorous
nightmares.

My computer
  died right after-
ward. I closed
  my eyes the way
you do when you
  have a migraine,
and jolted it open again . . .

The ancient Egyptians
  mixed ostrich
egg, bile, cypress
  bark and poured
the mixture on the face
  in order to smooth
out wrinkles. The word
  "cosmetics" means
  "to arrange
the cosmos" amid
  ruin. This is why
I inserted my
  credit card
into the slot
  and made sure
the machine felt
  my erotic, gold chip.

Having accidentally
  pressed Record
instead of Stop,
  I had long
forgotten the rules
  of this technology.
A squeal. Don't let
  this experience
scatter again, now
  that you are
gone forever.

Sheep-on-Ketamine
Study Reveals What
Happens When You
Fall Into a "K-Hole."

The lady who
  sold my face back
to me was not wearing
  her mask correctly.
It didn't matter.
  I marveled at her
delicate fingers
  fluttering like dollars
in the perfumed air
  of the deserted
department store.

The cassette
  sent to me asked
questions. Some
  were profound, others
were trivial. Why
do I feel so
  alone here
when the day is
  full of crossbills,
almost futuristic,
  bright and cold?
I texted him
  Are you feeling
better? and waited
  with the imperfect
knowledge of torn
  flags, gathering
more shells, spells
  refracting their
own allegorical
  properties as
object lessons.

The birdcalls
  were softer
at the start of
  the pandemic,
the creatures weren't
  as desperate to
overlap their notes,
  but as capital
learned new ways
  for traffic to pick up
the phenomenon
  gradually reversed
itself the way
  the instructions
from my son's
  science lesson
say to cut along
  the pencil line of
the Möbius strip
  lengthening the poem
indefinitely and what
  joy we took
in knowing there
  were still elemental
things like dyads
  (the interval
between notes),
  scripts on typewriter
ribbons at the Goodwill
  just waiting to be
read, rivers, factories
  of metaphor churning

I know such adorning
   is no real preparation
for death. Black
   nail polish is seldom
called black.
   It's called
Naughty Nails,
   Witch Witch, Things
I've Seen, Top
   Secret, Memento
Mori, Nuit.

It's hard to know
   what is left
when the moon
   glows red like this,
that debt collector
   squeezing a ball
of air in his hand.

"What am I worth?"
   the alchemist asks
deepening his
   gaze into the birth
chart, striking

a match as half
   the continent
is taken inward
   to flame, decorous
as emotions riding
   the haunting, "how
do I conjure?"

Now I know I should
take you back

to the polychrome
scene, but this

is just a screening.
Did you want things

to keep going forward?
I had a bad

feeling. It was
getting late. No one

was answering
the phone. The sinking

feeling wouldn't
go away. It was

eerie. By now
the cassette

tape was almost totally
erased. I wasn't

sure if it was in-
tentional or if I was

just a person full
of mistakes. The silence

went on
for many days.

I began to pull
the tape out of its shell.

It went on and on,
unspooling, un-

spolling with-
out sound.

out knowledge but
what I want to
   say here is that I don't
know how to love
   this place anymore

and everything I write
   seems to be a goodbye
to the little things
   I believed were what
made the place bearable—

adding currants
   to scones, even
a long run in
   the autumn on the green-

way that is now
   being metabolized
and bulldozed to make
   way for new housing.

I ran there and thought
   well, if I look the other
way, I will only
   feel what I want

to feel, that huge
   impending blush

sensation, waving
sea grasses beneath
the bodies
of seabirds.

On the Way to the Shore

I love and care
for people, even if

the social matrix
does everything in its crude

power to collapse
intense feeling, even

if every poem is subject
to gross humiliations.

*

Verging on the end,
my mouth is full of
antonyms,

so I place a robust
pot of flame-tip tulips

on the outdoor table
as the sea collects

its causalities, read
more frivolous articles:

. . . *much of the artwork
comes from people who are*

remodeling their beach cabins . . .
And from you: "I must

head off to a professional
development workshop."

These are the things we said
as the disaster took hold.

I Bought You a Bonsai

Containment zones
widen into spring

where bulbs are
flourishing
from the devastating
waters. Remember

your origin, says
the sea, ratcheting up
its chaotic philosophy.

I will hold you forever
since you are dearer

to me than a metaphor
dissolving its own letters.

Cypress Tree

Dawn begins in Florida's
opulent greenhouse.

This is nothing like
memory. It is the sound

of dripping, a Persephone
of vocative formulations.

This is no screen; it is
wood slowly rotting
on the forest floor

and the SIM-card-full-
sea calling out to be seen.

At Riverside
and Avondale,

past the marble house,
full of punctuation &
plants, deep where
the tornado untwines
its watch, what do you
want, Valentine? In
the shrine of sunshine,
    I lift my hoodie
over my life, pain
    scale 4, thought
your hands were pressed
to my face, but I am
walking into a glass
window, you in
Washington, prismatic
    but no water. *Is this
    landlocked person real?*
I ask my phone-synapses
strengthened by weed,
astrology, therapy,
and the Mute
button. You call from
    the capitol and I throw
my phone in the St.
John's River again.
    It's okay.
    You're used to it.

Let's get fucked up
    and forget the
pandemic, forget
the homicidal
    pantomimes with those
pretty pretties on screens
where you're supposed
to enact plenitude
    but sink so far into
    the orchestration
of money and shit.

It is the white flower
    that roars, oneirogenic,

a catastrophic tryst
    with undulating
cumulonimbus

clouds, the dripping of
water from a faun-shaped

fountain, happenstance
    in green, someone
vacuuming their

living room on a Sunday.
Oh love, I don't want

to see them anymore,
    the ghosts of my life,

of yours, can't our
    togetherness short-
circuit—?

But no. The refinery
    wavers, the men trickle

out with their lunch
boxes, where the salt wind
and chemicals

sting, sting, sting. It is not
    a dream. It is everything

you hoped to forget but
    couldn't. It is splashed
blood on the boardwalk

across from the oceanic
feeling you say you've

Why do men have
to kill the women they

can't possess in poems?
Like Richard Hugo's

"The Lady in Kicking
Horse Reservoir"—even

as sublimation, a sickness,

a devouring and devaluing
like that guy who tells you

*I love you I love you
I love you* and why do

the women in the 1980s
creative writing workshop

nod along to his
stupid story? No, you

don't love me, dickhead.
You just want your hands

to turn to weeds
so they can brush

my dead face
at the bottom of your lake.

How long will
I walk away into
   these lush hours;
the ones unspent
  in together's
  incarnadine never
did take the olive
   tree out of its bucket—
the leaves slowly
   fell off and I felt awful,
didn't have the heart
   to garden or compost
songs or disease, long
lists of foods I can
and cannot eat,
  the physical aspects:
crumbling, weight loss,
mysterious appearances: a
blue dress hanging from
   a low cloud, makeup
turning up in my mailbox
  shaped like a cottage—
  all the wrong colors
  but still applied them
diligently. Touchdown
  on Mars, the mail-
box collapsed, a 7th
grader biking
down the street
was jumped by three kids
I said, "do you want
   some water?" He was
crying I thought
don't look at me
like that please
don't look at me
like that. Like what?
Like an animal.

never experienced.

Well I have. I do.
Every day. I'm sorry I
can't help you.
I don't know how
to speak
the language of the dead.

ACKNOWLED

GMENTS

These poems appeared in the following publications, sometimes with different titles and in different forms:

The Account: "As in Leaving the Pyroclastic Volcano," "Dear Anselm,"
A) Glimpse) Of): "Double Happiness, or 'Modernity Means Contingency,'" "It Was Raining in the French Concession"
The American Poetry Review: "I Gave Birth in Another Era," "On the Way to the Shore I Bought You a Bonsai Cypress Tree," "Pastoral in the Minor Key"
Bennington Review: "Gong! Gong! Gong!," "Sketches for My Sweetheart the Drunk"
The Brooklyn Rail: "The Future Is No Longer What It Was," "Hold! Said the Hand Said the Money," "Now Wait for Last Year," "The Poet Enters through the Subjunctive Mood"
The Canary: "An Equanimous Defense of the Exclamation Point," "The Only Cloud in the Sky to Impress Me with a Demoniacal Grandeur," "With Joy with No Joy"
Chicago Review: "And the Days Shall Be Filled with Music," "Reading *The Bell Jar* in Everglades National Park"
Conduit: "Tick Tock Cryptic"
Couplet Poetry: "To Take a Lover in the Intricately Woven Kaleidoscope"
Green Mountains Review: "March Pandémie"
Guest: "Poem with Three Lines by Gustaf Sobin"
Kenyon Review: "Your Eyes Resemble Mine"
Lana Turner: "At Riverside and Avondale," "I Sang a Song with the Dead"
Poetry: "The Flammagenitus Strophes," "Let's Make the Water Turn Black"
Prelude: "Bildungsroman"
The Scales Project: "Now That You're Dead, I'm Observing Great Bodies of Water"

Thank you to the early readers of these poems especially to my pandemic writing group who helped me through the difficult months of 2020 and early 2021: Jon Riccio, Julie Phillips Brown, Alina Ştefă-nescu, Kimberly Quiogue Andrews, Jennifer Calkins, and Bill Neumire. Thank you to Summer J. Hart who collaborated with me to make the *11 Triptychs* chapbook. I will never forget sewing those 100 chapbooks together. Thank you to Michael Dumanis, Chris Nealon, Adrian Matejka, David Lau, Rodrigo Toscano, and Cal Morgan for your feedback and friendship, and to Matthew Zapruder and everyone at Wave Books. Deepest gratitude to Alex Papanicolopoulos for your love and fierce intelligence.